Keeping It Together: A Pa… Companion Through Decision-Making

By Sarah Fenlon Falk

Keeping It Together: A Patient's Companion Through Decision-Making

ISBN-13: 978-0-9994311-0-8
ISBN-10: 0-9994311-0-2

Cover art by Nikki Gauthier
Instagram @IntrospectiveLifeGirl
Email: IntrospectiveLifeGirl@gmail.com

TABLE OF CONTENTS

INTRODUCTION

If you're reading this book, chances are you and/or someone you love either has to or has had to make a major medical decision in your lifetime. Maybe you are seeking clarity for a decision you must make in the near future—or immediately. It is my hope that the journey I have been on, the path that I, and my mother before me, have forged, would prove to be of help and encouragement to you through what can seem like a medical maze.

I have been faced with major medical decisions before on multiple occasions and have been through the decision-making process with loved ones. In February 2015, I was diagnosed with stage 3 Her2+ breast cancer. This was not my first cancer diagnosis. In 1991, as a seventeen-year-old high school senior, I was diagnosed with osteogenic sarcoma in the left femur. I underwent 54 chemotherapy treatments in the course of a year at a hospital four and a half hours from home.

Being diagnosed as a teenager was a much different experience than being diagnosed as an adult. As an adult, it fell to me to make decisions. When I was a pediatric patient, I did what my parents told me to, who did what the doctors were telling them to do. We weren't educated on nutrition or complementary therapies at that time. We weren't given options. No one recommended a second opinion. In 1991 in Michigan, we were completely unaware of alternative treatments. I went through treatment then, a year of chemotherapy and limb-salvage/tumor removal surgery.

As months turned into years, the shadow that cancer had cast over my life, physically, emotionally, and spiritually, was forgotten. I worked my way through graduate school and began counseling cancer patients and their families/caregivers at a local cancer support center. I participated in cancer survivor events as keynote speaker, singer, and guest. I was able to make meaning of a situation that otherwise may have looked like pointless suffering. I was giving back and providing support to those who needed it most. In November of 2001, I received another medical diagnosis that forced me to educate myself and to make decisions for my health and treatment. The day before my twenty-eighth birthday I was diagnosed with diabetes. Because I did not meet the criteria for either Type I or Type II, the specifics of my diagnosis remained a mystery, which sent me on a journey for answers. Dumbfounded at first, I blindly took the medication prescribed by the diagnosing physician, a general practitioner. It was years before I was seen by an endocrinologist, which should have been the first thing recommended to me at the point of diagnosis. My roommate at the time, Kristi, had diabetes and she was a guide and support for me during those early days of managing diabetes. I also took it upon myself to read, seek medical opinions, and to ask a lot of questions. I tried different treatment options and have finally come to a place where I feel better about my diabetes care team and approach to management.

In January 2014, my family received a devastating blow. The mother who had driven me for treatment, my primary caregiver during the darkest time of my life to date, was herself diagnosed with cancer. She was diagnosed with estrogen receptive breast cancer, around stage 1. The reports had even suggested that the finding may be of a pre-cancerous nature, but nonetheless my mom was encouraged to have surgery as well as chemo or radiation treatment for added "insurance" against any possible recurrence. My mother declined all conventional medical advice and sought the knowledge, advice, and assistance of a naturopath she had been working with for years. This decision scared me. I remembered the arduous treatment regime I had encountered and endured in the 90s. It seemed my mother was taking the extreme opposite approach to her cancer. Initially it seemed to me that my mother was being quite cavalier, or perhaps that she was indifferent to the diagnosis. Against my better judgment, I had almost pleaded with her to at least have surgery. In retrospect, I know I reacted this way out of love, desperation and from a limited perspective.

> *I wanted to make that major medical decision for her because I didn't trust the choices she was making for herself.*

I wanted to pressure her into my way of thinking and believing about the situation. My mother was gracious with me as I pushed and pleaded with her about her decision. Over the next year, my mother and father taught those of us who watched them how to be patient; seek wise counsel from diverse sources; and to learn to trust one's own intuition regarding health and wellness. My mom managed her nutrition, took vitamins and supplements, used infrared hotbeds, and a chi machine. While her cancer was not gone, in a year's time she had held it at bay.

This approach may not be for everyone, but what it has taught me regarding making decisions and caring for myself is to ***take a pause***. To stop, breathe deeply, and reflect before undergoing any type of treatment.

I have taken this lesson to heart because in February 2015, I received another diagnosis, Her2 positive ductal carcinoma: breast cancer. I began to realize that the path my mother had forged granted me the luxury of easily accessible information, tried and proved methods for wellness, and ideas for a broader approach to this cancer diagnosis. Rather than simply (and somewhat blindly) following the medical doctor's recommendations, I sought integrative and alternative methods for dealing with cancer. During the process that I will take you through in this guide, I was able to make some

very difficult but necessary decisions. By no means was this an "easy" process, but some of the steps I took as laid out by my mother and as forged through my own searching have made the journey more manageable.
My mother continued to work with her cancer care team and eventually did undergo conventional treatment for her breast cancer. She and I are both doing well and have both been given the "all clear" from breast cancer. We both remain under the care of a surgeon for breast reconstruction. We also continue to see our oncologists and general practitioners. This follow-through and follow-up is very important in the continuing care of oneself even after the crisis is over.

If you have been recently diagnosed with cancer, or are facing a major medical decision of your own, it is my wish that you and your family/caregivers may be encouraged by my story.

> *Through sharing some of the things I've learned along the way, I hope to empower and even inspire you as you enter this season of serious discussions and decision-making.*

This book is meant to be marked up, written in, highlighted, carried to doctor appointments, earmarked, paper-clipped, and otherwise put through the paces on your behalf; put it to work! I hope it provides you with an outline for obtaining information from your own heart and mind as well as the necessary medical information you will need in making your decisions. I've left plenty of pages in the back for you to use as a notebook or journal. By learning and practicing some basic methods of relaxation, asking and answering several introspective questions, and through gathering and organizing information as it comes your way, I believe you will find your load lightened.

Beyond these basics, I hope you will find inspiration and meaning in the midst of your challenges and difficulty; that you will acknowledge your pain and struggle but also choose to see the miracles in the midst of it.

FIRST THINGS FIRST

1. Breathe Deeply

Relax. Take a deep breath. Just focus on the sound and feel of each breath you take. If you find this difficult, skip to page 41 and utilize the guided relaxation I've provided there. You could also practice taking a deep breath in through your nose for four counts, pausing with breath in for the count of five, and then exhaling for the count of eight. This will help you to calm your body, your nerves, and remind you how to breathe again. Having faced quite a few difficult medical decisions in my lifetime, I understand the whirlwind of thoughts and emotions that threaten to overtake a person. An assault on one's health is a stressful experience and in times of stress, our body is instinctively thrown into the stress response "fight, flight, or freeze." The body prepares itself to confront danger. Health problems can result if/when this stress response is left "on" for long periods of time, as can be the case with chronic stress.

The stress response suppresses the immune system, which in turn increases our susceptibility to illness. Taking time to catch your breath and learning to calm yourself will be a benefit to you—mind, body and spirit—in the coming days. There will be many intense moments, big conversations to be had, and plenty of stress that will leave you feeling at the very least weary. Deep breathing will serve to elicit the relaxation response in your body at times when you need it most.

Learning to breathe properly and knowing how to relax yourself will serve multiple purposes for you. The first we've already discussed: it will help your body to loosen and relax so that you don't remain in a perpetual state of tension. The next benefit may not be immediately apparent; however, as I teach all of my clients: focusing on your breathing, on relaxing your body, also provides you a moment to take control of your thoughts. When we are confronted with unwelcome news at our doctor's office, our mind starts to spin. Whether it is you or someone you love confronting this medical crisis head-on, the torrent of thoughts and fears can be overwhelming. Focusing on your breathing shifts stressful thoughts, which threaten to intrude your every waking moment, to something therapeutic for your wellbeing.

Another benefit of deep breathing, or abdominal breathing: it completes the full oxygen exchange in the lungs—incoming oxygen and outgoing carbon dioxide. We typically breathe quite shallowly and the lowest part of our lungs doesn't get a fair share of oxygenated air. This can make you feel short of breath. Using deep abdominal breathing techniques can slow the heartbeat and serve to lower or stabilize blood pressure.

Breathing deeply and properly takes practice and attention. When I teach deep breathing to my clients in my private counseling practice, I begin with the diaphragm. Any singer or musician who plays a wind instrument knows all about the diaphragm. Imagine a little balloon fixed just below and at the center of your rib cage and at the top of your belly. When you take a deep breath in through your nose, you will want to send that breath right down to fill up that balloon. So with the deep breath, your belly will rise before your chest does. You will fill up your diaphragm, then your lungs. Once the diaphragm and lungs are full, pause, and then slowly exhale. You may choose to exhale through your nose. I prefer exhaling through the mouth; however, more moisture is lost when exhaling through the mouth.

Your exhale should be longer than your inhale. When you exhale, be sure to release any and all of the air out. Remember, the goal is for a full oxygen exchange; we want to clear out the lungs.

Let's practice this together now:

Close your eyes.

Turn your attention to your breathing. You may notice that it is shallow and rapid. Perhaps your breathing is light and weak.

In a moment you will begin to breathe deeply, but first, imagine your diaphragm, a tiny balloon located just below your ribcage.

When you take your deep breath, imagine the breath going to your diaphragm, filling it up, and then filling your lungs.

Now imagine that as you exhale the air from your lungs and diaphragm, you will be releasing any tension or anxiety that has been held within your body.

You will breathe in calm and peace.

You will exhale anxiety and tension.

Now it's time to begin to breathe deeply.

Breathe in through your nose down into your diaphragm.

Fill up your diaphragm and lungs.

Pause. 1 2 3.

Now slowly exhale through your mouth, blowing away all tension.

And breathe normally.

Repeat this as many times as necessary until you feel your jaw and shoulders relax and/or feel a deeper sense of calm and peace of mind. It doesn't solve the problem but it creates a frame of mind that is now able to approach it.

> *Caring for the mind and body beyond a medication or treatment that your doctor prescribes is essential to living well; to not only surviving a medical crisis but thriving in the midst of it.*

2. The Power of Organization

One of the first things my mom did when I was diagnosed in 1991 as a seventeen-year-old was to start a folder of all pertinent medical information. So, when I was diagnosed again as a forty-one-year-old, I did the same. **Find a notebook or journal and plan on carrying it with you for a while. A folder or binder can be helpful as well, to keep paperwork or lab reports in. You may choose to use this workbook as your journal, which would be great. It was created with that use in mind!**

Through the years, I've learned to ask for copies of all of my tests once they are completed. Some facilities and offices set patients up on a patient portal or other system that allows them access to their medical records online. Since I'm a hands-on person and don't have the capacity to remember various different log in names and passwords, I prefer to have a hard copy and keep each report in a binder. It's simpler for me if I have it to hold, information at my fingertips. But do what works best for you. If you'd prefer to keep track of portal user names and passwords, feel free to utilize the last page of this workbook for that purpose. (**A page has also been provided for a list of your medications**!) The point is to have all of your medical info in one spot and in a place that is easily accessible to you.

If you are seeking a second opinion, very often the new doctor will want to see the actual scans/x-ray/slides/etc., so it is always a good idea to ask for those at the time of service so you don't have to make an extra trip or have to add another thing to your to-do list.

Another very important purpose for your notebook is to write down any and all questions that you may have for your doctor. It's important not to depend on your memory for anything at this point. Your fears or frustrations can skew the information you are receiving as well as cause you to forget any or all of the questions you may have had in mind before your appointment. Not only that, but you might be working with a number of doctors at any given time and it will be beneficial for you to keep all information organized and clear. This is especially helpful when you are seeking 2nd (or 3rd) opinions.

I kept a notebook with me to take notes at all appointments, and I also kept a binder for all of my test results. I used a tab system according to type of test and which hospital/doctor so that I could keep it all straight: who said or did what.

I'll tell you what, I am a list person. If it's not written down in black and white, it either didn't happen or it's not going to. When under a large amount of stress, oftentimes we become scattered and find it difficult to focus. We forget what we are trying to say, we forget appointments, don't ask questions we meant to ask, take too much or not enough of that one pill, and haven't filled the script for that other medication yet either. It's easy to get all tangled up in information, questions you may have, and tasks that need to be done. So in this book I've tried to make it easy for you. I've formatted this area after my own journaling system. I encourage you to try out this very simple record-keeping system and see if it works for you. If it does—great! If not, feel free to customize it. It needs to make sense to you so that you can use it to manage the information and question overload.

After the informational portion of this book I have formatted the remaining pages so that you can utilize the rest of the pages for recordkeeping. You will find a section for doctor appointments, test results, and planning. I hope you will find it useful.

3. Gain Perspective: Getting to Know You

While much of the medical care in our society today is standardized, you will find not all doctors and their beliefs or approaches to be so. While a second opinion may at first suggestion seem redundant, you will soon find that there is value in it. But before searching for a second opinion, take another deep breath.

> *It's time for some introspection. No need to dig too deeply. This will be something you already know about yourself but perhaps haven't considered in quite this specific way.*

Ask yourself the following questions and allow yourself some time to consider:

What do I believe about healing?

This is very important to consider. Think about how you have dealt with illness in the past. Have you been one to beeline to the medicine cabinet to take an ibuprofen for an ache or a Tylenol for fever? Or do you tend to increase your fluid intake and vitamin C for said symptoms? Maybe you fall somewhere in between.

I saw a quote somewhere and have been unable to find it again. The gist of it was that our body does not know the name of particular disease; it simply knows something is out of balance. In our culture, when we hear the word "cancer," we are typically struck with fear or dread. Some of us experience an anxiety attack due to our history with the disease. After all, cancer impacts a majority of our population. So, the question for you is, despite the identity of the disease, what do you believe about treating illness?

What do you believe about healing? Once you are able to answer this question, you may already know what you will need or want to do. Also, your point of view on the matter may change as you gather information, weigh options, and hear stories of how others have healed themselves.

What do you believe about healing?

What are my spiritual beliefs?

Spiritual beliefs directly impact attitude. When healing is the goal, a positive attitude is imperative. Take another deep breath in through your nose, filling up your diaphragm and lungs. Pause. Now slowly exhale through your mouth as if you're blowing all stress, tension, and confusion away. Now consider this question again: *What are my spiritual beliefs?* When I was diagnosed with cancer for the second time in my life, I was shocked. I felt as though I had paid my dues to this disease and could not believe I had to face it once again. **But in my heart and soul I also knew that trials and hardships aren't meaningless.** It is my firm belief that there is a God and that He works all things for good. Since my understanding of my life and this world is so limited, I see but a tiny puzzle piece; so I have to put my faith in a God whom I believe sees the big picture. I knew that if this, if cancer, was happening to me again, there must be purpose behind it. Because of this belief I was able to find meaning in the midst of another cancer diagnosis. I decided that I would share the inspiration and empowerment that I received on this journey.

I have tried to remain positive throughout my health crisis and have found beauty in the midst of pain.
Most books or research I've read speak to the necessity of a positive attitude in the midst of a personal crisis for the benefit of healing, treatment efficacy, or a more positive personal experience.

You can see then how this is a very important question to ask yourself. Maybe you are clear on what your spiritual beliefs are but you're too angry or scared to lean into your beliefs at this time. Or perhaps you're questioning your beliefs. After all, how could a loving God allow such horrible things? I've written about this very topic. In my book *Finding Myself…Facing Cancer,* I wrote a chapter called "Productive Partners, Faith and Doubt." This was composed while I was facing a breast cancer diagnosis and treatment. I worked through some of the fear and doubt that had been crippling me in my decision-making process. I came to the conclusion that faith and doubt, these two elements, often move us forward. I wrote:

"Faith and doubt are not polar opposites. Faith and certainty may be more so. It wasn't certainty that propelled Peter out of the boat onto the stormy sea but rather faith in the Savior standing on the waves. (Matthew 14:22-33)

Faith and doubt go hand in hand to motivate us to dig deeper, seek answers, take another step, go further, work harder, and to trust with reckless abandon.

I'm glad that I understand this about faith and doubt because as I stand with my feet planted on the deck of the boat and the stormy sea rages about me, I am quite uncertain. What was excitement last week at finalizing a treatment plan and preparing to get things started has turned into anxious energy this week. My stomach is sending me a twisted message and I'm feeling seasick. Deep breathe in. Exhale slowly. Yes, I've been practicing my deep breathing and my visualization, imagining chemotherapy as an army sent to war on my behalf to wipe out the enemy. I've been visualizing the healthy cells in my body being protected from the battle and growing in strength. I've visualized the room where I'll receive my treatments and have seen God Himself there with open arms to hold me in these hours."

For me, it was important to acknowledge that I was having doubts concerning God's presence in the midst of my pain and that I was experiencing anxiety regarding my treatment decisions. Once I was able to speak about how I was feeling, I could sort through the thoughts and emotions to find my way forward in the process.

It is vital to consider where you stand emotionally and spiritually. This will help to guide you in your decision making and will also allow you to seek strength and support from an outside source rather than relying on yourself for all that you will need for each step.

Conversely, this question may pose a challenge for you. Perhaps you've envisioned a god or higher power that is a taskmaster, expecting much from you, or a judge who simply doles out judgment and punishment. When I was diagnosed at age 17, I wondered what I had done wrong, what I had done to deserve such a harsh sentence. But through time, questioning, and seeking, I came to find that I was not being punished. The fact that I live in a world where there is sickness and disease simply means it could happen to me. And it did. And it has happened to you too. Consider what your narrative, your deep-seeded beliefs, and your belief in God, a higher power, or the universe, are so that you can work through any negative or inaccurate views you may have.

Many times we project on God
the judgment or self-loathing that we feel toward ourselves.
Once we take the time to address this,
then we can heal from the inside out.

What are your spiritual beliefs? What are some things you may need to work out within yourself so you can move toward spiritual wellness?

STAGES OF DECISION MAKING

Through my time seeking out the best possible treatment for my breast cancer, I realized I was following the example my mother set out for me and tweaking it a bit to suit my personality and needs. I wrote down my process as I went along in hopes of being able to use it later as well as to offer what I had learned to others. This is my process; I hope you find it useful:

1. Build Your Team

Ask yourself, "Who do I know?" You've already considered your own point of view regarding healing, the treatment of illness, and your spiritual beliefs. You know where you stand, so now you can begin to build your team. Your team will be those people who are going to manage your care as long as you need to address this illness in your body/life. These people will not only be healthcare or wellness professionals but also people who are there for emotional and informational support; doctors, nurses, naturopaths, nutritionists, pastors, friends, and other patients who have been where you are now.

Ask yourself if you know someone (and chances are you do) who has received the same or a similar diagnosis, someone you could talk to or approach with specific questions. This can be especially valuable if you are close to this person and respect them.

When I was diagnosed with cancer in February 2015, I had friends connecting me with their friends who were breast cancer survivors. It was one such connections, one woman in particular, whose input turned out to be of utmost encouragement and enlightenment for me. We shared similar family structure, life experiences, faith base, and diagnosis: Her2 positive ductal carcinoma. And her knowledge as a nurse was a bonus!

Use the lines below to write down ideas of those you may want on your team:

2. Gather Information

This step is about asking as many questions as you can think to ask. For some people, this is a foreign concept. "Doctors should never be questioned" seems to be a common thought in some circles. But it's important to obtain the specifics of your particular medical issue. For instance, there are many types of cancers and many qualifiers within each cancer type. Breast cancer isn't simply "breast cancer" but is classified by tumor receptor, tumor size, and location(s). Diabetes comes in types, Type I and Type II, with different types and categories still being researched.

Asking questions is an important step in informed decision-making. Here are some questions for you to consider. Should any of these topics apply to you, please highlight, underline, or write them down in the lines below to ask at your next appointment:

Should your diagnosis be treated with urgency rather than as an emergency?

For instance, if you have been diagnosed with cancer, the tumor you discovered did not develop overnight. It has taken much time to grow into what it is today. Typically, hours, days or sometimes even weeks (depending on the type of cancer) won't change the stage of the cancer or treatment outcomes. This fact works in your favor. It will give you time to gather your facts. Chances are, not every clinical question was answered with biopsy alone. If you've had more testing done—PET scan, MRI, CT scan, ultrasound, x-rays, blood work, etc.—then you may be starting out with more of the pertinent information needed to make next-step decisions. There are certain questions that should be answered early on in your diagnosis. If your doctor is unable to answer these questions, then perhaps more testing will need to be ordered. (For more information on the specific information these tests provide, see the Glossary at the end of this book.)

The following questions are focused around a cancer diagnosis. But if you are facing another type of diagnosis, you can use the same questions in your information-gathering process. Simply replace the word "cancer" with your diagnosis and see if it fits. I have also provided alternate questions to ask.

If you have been diagnosed with cancer, however, here are some questions that will be important to have answers to:

What stage is the cancer?

Cancer is staged from 0 (yes, pre-cancerous polyps, cells, clusters, anything that holds strong potential for turning cancerous is staged on the cancer continuum) to stage 4. Stage 4 cancer is also known as metastatic cancer, meaning the cancer has spread from its primary site/original location and has gone to other areas of the body. For example, if a woman is diagnosed with Stage 4 breast cancer with mets (short for metastasis) to the lung, that means her original cancer has spread. She does not have breast and lung cancer. Treatment recommendations will typically be more aggressive in higher stages of cancer.

What stage is the cancer? Or, how far has this health issue progressed?

Write down any questions you may have regarding the stage or progression of your diagnosis:

____

____

____

____

____

____

____

Where is the primary location of the cancer?

This is an issue for someone with a stage 4 cancer. For instance, if a man bothered by back pain is found to have a tumor on his spine but a PET scan shows he has a tumor in his left lung as well, the primary source of his cancer may be the lung. Lung cancer will be treated differently than bone cancer would. Thus, the location of the primary tumor is necessary to determine.

Where is the primary location of the cancer? Or, what are the areas of involvement particular to my diagnosis?

____

____

____

____

____

What are other important characteristics of this tumor?

This question is a necessary one for the woman diagnosed with breast cancer. Breast cancer tumors have different receptors, meaning they feed off certain elements the body produces. Receptors can be hormones, estrogen, or progesterone, or Her2 receptor, which is a protein. There are targeted therapies available, which aim to block these receptors, deeming it necessary to determine the receptor fueling the tumor.

Another example of why this question is important to answer is the fact that there are over 120 different types of brain cancer. Again, in the case of brain cancer, the exact type of tumor will be necessary to determine so that treatment options can be properly discussed.

What are other important characteristics of this tumor? Or of my diagnosis?

____

____

____

____

____

When gathering information, you will be given a lot of numbers and statistics. There can be an inclination to go all-in where those statistics are concerned. There will be much talk in the coming days of diagnosis, the name and specifics of your cancer or other diagnosis, as well as prognosis (probability of recovery) with certain treatments. While this information is based on research and experience, it is valuable in a sweeping sense. Let me be more specific and clear: You are an individual. There is no one else in this world like you. You are a perfectly designed original. There is no one else with the same metabolism, height, weight, immune system, allergies, and sensitivities all in the same package. Because of this, I say that research is only valuable in a general sense; because there is no one else in the world like you, you may not respond in the same way to treatment as others have. You may or may not experience side effects the way the majority did. No one else receiving the standardized treatment has the same body, is on the same medications, has the same medical history, and etc., as you. Therefore, this information is best taken in the perspective of a broad scope rather than as a rule.

It's important to remember, as you are considering all these facts and figures, a truth learned in childhood, that in this life there are no guarantees. We do what we can to cover our bases, perform our due diligence, maintain our responsibilities, but in the end, it is what it is. For some this is freeing, for others, frightening. I say this to encourage you.

If you are looking over information and the statistics say one thing but your gut is saying something else, listen to both.
Don't get too hung up on the numbers.
The numbers are not guarantees.

I'd like to share a journal entry that addresses information overload. Written December 1, 2015, I titled the entry "Filter, Balance, Breathe." While our search for information in our treatment is a good thing, it can become overwhelming. This was the point I had come to when writing this. I hope the approach I took to the information overload will help you to manage it as well:

"In my quest to learn and formulate a strategy for health and disease prevention, I have become overwhelmed with information. Not only that, but as I share what I'm reading and learning, I have come to realize that this is becoming overwhelming for some of my friends and family. Especially in the area of nutrition, there are so many ideas out there as to what is the best way to feed the body. If you look at the bookstore or do an online search for 'diet,' 'nutrition,' or the like, you will find many differing opinions. There are articles on topics that go beyond simply what to eat and offer weight-loss and health solutions regarding how often, when, and how to eat. (Paying attention to your food does assist in digestion, so I'm not knocking the 'how' here; I'm just proving the point that all this information can be overwhelming!)

"I'm sorry if you've become confused or overwhelmed with me in this process! If you have, I'd like to share what I've learned to do throughout my search. With all of this information I have two choices: to **filter it** or **file it**. If a particular article or topic seems a little far-fetched to me from the get-go, I will filter that one. But, if I read a book or a study that makes a lot of sense to me intuitively and provides practical tips for real life, then I will most certainly file it. So, just remember as you're trying to sort through all of my posts, Facebook shares, and tweets that if the information does not seem to fit into your mindset or lifestyle, keep what you can from the info and let the rest go. Filter or file it.

"The next point I want to be sure to make about this info overload is the idea of balance. Balance the time you spend reading or looking into health and wellness issues. Sometimes too much information is simply that: too much information. I've begun to realize I really need to put a cap on how much time I allow myself to spend searching or reading about prevention and wellness, even though that is my crusade at the moment. If I spend too much time on this, I am neglecting other things in my life that are also necessary for my health such as solitude, quality time with my family and friends, time for creativity, and so on. I don't want to be up in my head all the time, with my nose in a book or eyes glued to a computer screen reading up on my diagnosis and treatment options. I need to feel the sun on my face, move around a bit, and listen to the stories and laughter of my children.

What I have found in this process is that I have produced stress within myself by overanalyzing food, wellness, and prevention. This has begun to outweigh the good of the information I've been gathering. I've taken steps toward establishing boundaries through the 'filter it/file it' system and then by remembering to seek a balance in my life. But it is time for me to take boundaries a step further with myself in regards to the information overload. I must step back and evaluate what I do know, then move ahead."

It's time to step back and evaluate what you know from the information you've gathered, then, move forward.

Are there any other questions you'd like answered regarding your diagnosis?

Write them in the spaces below and ask them at your next appointment:

3. Create a Plan

So, you've been practicing taking deep, cleansing breaths when you feel tension rising within you. You've spent time gathering information specific to your diagnosis. You have considered your personal position regarding healing and the role of your spiritual beliefs and attitude. You've probably talked to some people who have been through your diagnosis and the proposed treatment already. And you've taken some time to get organized with all that you've learned in this process.

Now it's time to weed through all that you have in front of you. This is all information you will need to make decisions going forward. These are decisions you will make with your heart **and** your head.

I was blessed with supportive and open-minded family and friends who understood the importance of allowing me to make my own decisions. No one pressured me to choose a certain path. Many made their opinions quite clear, but also made certain that it was not imposed upon me. Ultimately, I, with those closest to me, sought peace when choosing a path or plan. It would be no surprise to me if patients were found to fare better and respond better to treatment when they feel empowered, when they feel they have been listened to and have been the captain of their own ship, so to speak. You must believe in the path you have chosen. So seek peace with every step. An important part of this inner peace is being able to trust your intuition.

Perhaps you've struggled with being indecisive in the little things of life such as where to go to dinner, what to wear, and which color or pattern of towel to purchase. You're not alone in this struggle. If this is an issue for you at this point, I'd like you to consider the amount of time and effort you have put into this process already.

You've gathered your information, asked your questions and now it's time to contemplate a few more things:

What feels right?

You've examined what you know. Now, given all that you have in front of you, what simply *feels* best to you? Envision yourself a mile or two down that road, a month or so into any given scenario. Which scenario makes the most sense to you? Which choice seems the most true to who you are as a person? Which path seems the most authentic, a way you might typically respond? Only you hold the answers to these questions. Sometimes it is helpful to ask one or two people closest to you to help with reflection, but ultimately, these are answers you hold within you.

____

____

____

____

____

____

____

____

Who is already on my team?

Throughout this process, you have gathered those people around you who have aided you in your quest for medical information and for personal enlightenment. These people have been there to encourage you, remind you about the strength you forgot you possess, and to help you gather facts so you can consider your options. This is your team: the medical personnel, the family members, the friends, and coworkers. Recall those who have been most instrumental in this process thus far.

Which specialist, surgeon, or nurse really seemed to understand where you are coming from? Who took the most time to listen to your concerns?

Determining this can help you choose the direction for your care. Perhaps these people will become permanent members of your team and integral to your healing.

What have your family members and friends been saying to you?

They won't always think the same way that you do, but who has shown the grace and patience you've needed while seeking out the right path?

____

____

____

____

____

> *These are people to keep about you*
> *as you begin a long journey toward healing.*
> *You will need much patience and grace during this time.*
> *People who exhibit these gifts will help remind you*
> *to treat yourself with kindness.*

4. Follow-Through

It's time to proceed with your people to the place where you'll carry out your plan! Those you've chosen to be on your team will help support you through your treatment; they may even be giving you rides; the medical and wellness people on your team will be providing the treatment and updating the plan as things progress.

Follow-through may sound self-explanatory but anyone who has ever made a treatment plan, birth plan, vacation plan, party plan, visitation plan (you get the idea)—anyone who has ever planned anything knows that even best-laid plans rarely go 100% according to the notes. So, while it is important to go to your appointments, follow your nutrition plan, maintain your medication, get enough sleep, taking notes all the while, it's also important to remember that things may change up as you go.

Using the space below, list some potential obstacles in following through with your treatment plan (e.g., transportation issues, forgetting medications, access to the treatment you require, finances, etc.). Once you've made your list, go back and consider possible solutions (e.g., friends with cars, alarms for reminders, alternative treatment methods, family fundraisers, etc.):

Obstacles:	Solutions:
______________________	______________________
______________________	______________________
______________________	______________________
______________________	______________________
______________________	______________________
______________________	______________________
______________________	______________________
______________________	______________________
______________________	______________________
______________________	______________________
______________________	______________________
______________________	______________________

5. Follow-Up

While Follow-Up may sound redundant coming after Follow-Through, it is different. Similar in that it will require you to go to your appointments, follow your nutrition plan, maintain your medication, get enough sleep, taking notes all the while, but this is for the long haul. You've followed-through with treatment, now it's a matter if maintaining or "keeping up" the good habits you've developed as you learn to take better care of yourself. This is the point where the intensity of the crisis may have passed and now you have been instructed to continue seeing your doctor, nutritionist, etc. for maintenance.

Unfortunately, it is in this stage when your friends and family may be taking a sigh of relief as if to say, "Ah. It's all over."
But, it is not "over".

I know for myself, having been diagnosed with cancer for a second time, I am more worried since finishing treatment than I was while I was in it. At least when I was in active treatment I felt like I was addressing my diagnosis head-on. Now that I am beyond treatment and don't have the community of support around me quite so tightly, I feel anxious. Not only that, but maintaining the steps taken to become well can be trying and tiring. You may have to be more proactive in gathering your team and getting the support you need to follow-up. But don't be shy. If you must, you can remind them from time to time that while the crisis is over, there are still things you are managing and could use their support with. Be direct and honest about what you need. Just ask for help.

What if it comes back? is a question I commonly ask, and I am certain I am not alone. You may be thinking, *right, what if it happens again?* And all I can tell myself or you is that if it comes back, if it happens again, then we will deal with it. Until then, we focus on being well. We focus on caring for ourselves: mind, body, and spirit, not neglecting any part of ourselves, because we know what neglect produces.

> *So for the long haul we keep gathering information on how to care for our changing body.*

We remain as active as we can. We eat those foods that we know feed our body, not disease. As part of our newfound wellness, we meditate, pray, or keep a gratitude journal. All these things we will use as we recreate our life. Because anyone who has ever had a major life event knows that once you've lived through it, life will never be the same.

Use the space below to write out those measures you've taken and will continue toward your health and wellness. Make a note of that member of your team who would support you in the steps that seem overwhelming.

6. Recreate

Because life will never be the same again after this, you will be creating and settling into your "new normal." Depending on what you've been through, even your body may look different to you. You may have less physical capabilities than you had before your medical crisis. Perhaps the treatment you require is ongoing and you will have routine appointments for the rest of your life. Whatever the case, it may be true for you that these changes are not easy. It's not as though you tried a new hairstyle because you wanted something new but can let it grow out, or bought an outfit just for the fun of it but kept the receipt in case you wanted to return it. This was an undesirable event and the aftermath leaves you trying to make sense of your life now.

When I was diagnosed with bone cancer as a senior in high school, I had all kinds of plans and ideas for my life that were rendered impossible after having part of my femur removed and a titanium rod placed into my leg. Before that I had run track, played soccer, cheered for basketball, wanted to run cross-country, and thought about going into the Air Force. After cancer, I was not able to do any of those things. I had to find a new direction and focus for my life. I had to recreate my life, in essence.

It took me many years to find my way and to bloom into what I was A.C. (After Cancer). I ventured in many different directions and tried to find my way to what I could identify with in my new body, with my new limitations and new anxiety about sickness and death. But eventually I found my way. Music replaced sports for me. I learned to play the guitar, began leading worship on mission trips and at church.

At first I had depended upon others to guide my re-creation and found myself in many dead-end relationships, both friendships and romantic relationships, as a result. I was trying to find my place in the world but didn't know how to go about it. Eventually, I went back to college, earned both a bachelor's degree as well as a master's degree, began working, and felt a sense of purpose once again. It wasn't until then that I met the man who would be my husband. Now as a wife and mother to four young boys, I have a distinct sense of purpose and focus in my life. This focus and identity helped me get through my treatment and now propels me forward, reminding me to care for myself, to live well, and to thrive in the midst of and beyond these life changes.

Use the space below to write about those things that you will have to give up due to this health crisis. Then write out the things you are still able to do. Next add things to your list those things you've always wanted to do but haven't done yet.

Had to give up:

Am still able to do:

Have always wanted to (and now I can/will!):

7. Thrive

Prosper. Flourish. Bloom. Do well. These are all definitions of the word *thrive*. Once you've gone through a life-changing event, it transforms you and can grow you into someone more empathetic, knowledgeable, mindful, and focused. I've already explained to you how my life-changing event first sent me on a wild goose chase for my identity, then sent me into panic attacks due to worry over its return. But I have learned to manage my anxiety, found purpose and passion in places I had not found them before, and have made a truly beautiful life from it. It's not what I had envisioned, nor is it what was planned, but for me it is perfectly imperfect. I wouldn't change a thing.

I'm at a place now where I know there are still areas for growth and that in order to thrive, to be a healthier, happier version of myself, I must give up more (e.g., junk food, staying up late). These are small sacrifices for being well, for blooming and flourishing.

So while the crisis may be over for you, or perhaps your diagnosis was not of an acute disease but rather a chronic one, then you understand the need to grab hold of this new normal and run with it so you can thrive in the midst of and beyond your diagnosis.

Your diagnosis does not define you.
It may have become a part of your life as "cancer-survivor"
has become a part of mine, but that is not who we are at our core.
There is so much more to you and I.
Remember we are caring for mind, body and spirit
and our diagnosis is a small part of that.

In the space provided below, write about those areas of your life where you wish to thrive:

RESOURCES

While I have outlined for you ways to quiet your mind and center in on your true beliefs about treatment and healing, and listed steps in decision-making as well as the differing stages of managing illness and recovery, I want to leave you with a list of resources that you may find beneficial. This is not an exhaustive list by any means. I want to provide you with a diverse variety of resources and ones that were specifically helpful to me. These may serve as a springboard for your personal research. Much of the information is regarding integrative and alternative approaches. I provide these because you will most likely be inundated with information for conventional treatment such as chemotherapy, radiation and surgery. I don't exclude information on conventional treatments as a way to state an opinion about what course of action you should take. I myself went through chemotherapy and surgeries. I simply found some information was not as easily accessible and wanted to provide it to you to spare you some of the work. Much of my research is cancer related due to my own experience.

www.health.harvard.edu Harvard Health Publications from the Harvard Medical School. Organized site with understandable information provided. Anything from relaxation techniques to the latest medical research can be found here.

www.radicalremission.com Born from the book *Radical Remission,* this website provides first hand accounts of those who have survived even the most grim of cancer diagnoses and how they healed. This book really encouraged me during my decision-making and treatment process.

www.kelly-turner.com Dr. Kelly Turner wrote the book *Radical Remission* based on thousands of interviews.

www.lifeovercancer.com Dr. Keith Block, author of *Life Over Cancer* and founder of The Block Center for Integrative Cancer Treatment where I received my chemotherapy treatment, shares information from research and professional/personal experience. You can learn more about The Block Center for Integrative Cancer Treatment on this site as well.

www.chrisbeatcancer.com Chris Wark shares his experience with colon cancer and his chosen method(s) of healing and treatment as well as the extensive research he has done in this area. The website also provides interviews with other cancer survivors.

www.cancer.org The American Cancer Society. This website provides statistics and some research- and diagnosis-specific information.

www.pubmed.gov Search many diagnoses, treatments, and topics in government research articles here.

www.cancertutor.com This website provides information on many integrative and alternative cancer treatments as well as explanation of different cancer types.

www.mercola.com Dr. Mercola is an alternative medicine doctor practicing out of Chicago, IL.

www.cancer.net It provides an excellent glossary of medical terminology.

100 Perks of Having Cancer: Plus 100 Health Tips for Surviving it, by Florence Strang and Susan Gonzalez

Dr. Jensen's Nutrition Handbook, by Dr. Bernard Jensen

Prayers from the Heart, by Richard J. Foster

Radical Remission, by Dr. Kelly Turner

www.sarahfenlonfalk.com I share information from my own research, experience and insights from my journey of growth and healing. I also published a book based on my blogs, *Finding Myself…Facing Cancer*, in 2017.

GLOSSARY
of Medical Terms

BIOPSY is a medical procedure that, for most types of cancer, is the only way to make a definitive cancer diagnosis, because it provides the most accurate analysis of tissue. Based on this analysis, the pathologist determines whether the tissue that was removed contains a tumor and whether this tumor is benign (noncancerous) or malignant (cancerous, meaning that it can spread to other parts of the body).
The types of biopsies include:
Fine needle aspiration biopsy
Core needle biopsy
Assisted biopsy
Image-guided biopsy
Surgical biopsy
There are two main categories of surgical biopsies:
- An incisional biopsy removes a piece of the suspicious area for examination.
- An excisional biopsy removes the entire lump.

Endoscopic biopsy
Bone marrow biopsy

BONE SCAN is an imaging test that uses a very small amount of a radioactive substance (tracer) to find or monitor cancer that started in the bones or that has spread to the bones from another part of the body.

CT, computed tomography, (also known as a "CAT" scan) is a scan that creates a three-dimensional picture of the inside of the body with an X-ray machine. A computer then combines these images into a detailed, cross-sectional view that shows any abnormalities or tumors. Sometimes a contrast or dye is injected into a patient's vein to create more detail in the images. One risk of this test is radiation exposure, especially for children. However, the potential benefits of having a CT scan usually outweigh these risks. If you are receiving multiple CT scans and x-rays, though, talk with your doctor about whether another type of test that involves less exposure to radiation can be done.

MRI, magnetic resonance imaging, is a test that uses magnetic fields, not X-rays, to produce detailed images of the body, helping a doctor find, evaluate, or monitor a cancer. During an MRI, a special dye may be used to help create a clearer picture. Because it does not use X-rays or other forms of radiation, an MRI is often used to look for problems in the female and male reproductive systems. In addition, it is often used to look for and evaluate tumors in the chest and abdomen, including in the breast.

MUGA, a multigated acquisition scan, creates video images of the ventricles (lower chambers of the heart that hold blood) to check whether they are pumping blood properly. It shows any abnormalities in the size of the ventricles and in the movement of the blood through the heart.

PET, positron emission tomography scan, is a diagnostic tool used to detect cancer and find out the cancer's stage. Knowing the cancer's stage helps you and your doctor decide what kind of treatment is best and helps predict prognosis. The scan can also be used to evaluate the effectiveness of cancer treatments, such as chemotherapy or radiation therapy.

PET-CT scan combines images from a positron emission tomography (PET) scan and a computed tomography (CT) scan that have been performed at the same time using the same machine. Because a CT scan provides detailed pictures of tissues and organs inside the body, while a PET scan reveals any abnormal activity that might be going on there, combining these scans creates a more complete image than either test can offer alone.
One risk of this test is radiation exposure. Although it is minimal for the PET scan portion of the test because the radioactive substance only remains in your body for a short time, there is more radiation exposure associated with the CT scan. Usually the potential benefits of the test outweigh these risks.

TUMOR MARKERS (also known as BIOMARKERS) are substances found at higher than normal levels in the blood, urine, or body tissue of some people with cancer. Although cancer cells often produce tumor markers, other healthy cells in the body produce them as well.
Along with other diagnostic tests, testing for tumor markers can indicate the presence of cancer and help doctors make treatment decisions. Tumor markers are most commonly used to do the following:
Screen high-risk individuals
Confirm the diagnosis
Predict prognosis
Guide treatment decisions
Monitor treatment
Predict or monitor for recurrence

ULTRASOUND, also called SONOGRAPHY or ULTRASONOGRAPHY, is an imaging test that uses high-frequency sound waves to create a picture of internal organs. The sound waves hit the organs and then bounce back to a device called a transducer that turns them into images and displays them on a computer monitor for the doctor to examine. Abnormal growths of tissue create different echoes of the sound waves than healthy tissue, so a doctor is able to detect a potential tumor. Ultrasound is also used to help a doctor perform a biopsy (the removal of a small amount of tissue for examination under a microscope) by showing a tumor's exact location in the body.

For a more exhaustive list of medical testing for cancer visit www.cancer.net

For a glossary of medical terms find the Harvard Medical Dictionary at https://www.health.harvard.edu/a-through-c

GUIDED RELAXATION

Start by placing your feet flat on the floor.
Sit back and allow the chair/couch to hold you.
If you are on your bed, lie flat and feel your whole body being held by the bed.
Good.
Now close your eyes.
Turn your attention to your breathing.
You may notice that it is shallow and rapid.
Perhaps your breathing is light and weak.
In a moment you will begin to breathe deeply, but first, imagine your diaphragm, a tiny balloon located just below your ribcage.
When you take your deep breath, imagine the breath going to your diaphragm, filling it up, then going into your lungs to fill them up.
Now imagine that when you exhale the air from your lungs and diaphragm you will be releasing any tension or anxiety that has been held within your body.
You will breathe in calm and peace.
You will exhale anxiety and tension.
Now it's time to begin to breathe deeply.
Breathe in through your nose down into your diaphragm.
Fill up your diaphragm and now your lungs.
Pause.
Now slowly exhale through your mouth, blowing away all tension.
Breathe normally.
Ready to take another deep breath, in through your nose, down into your diaphragm.
Good.
Filling up your lungs and pause.
Now slowly exhale through your mouth.
Feel how your jaw, shoulders, abdomen, and thighs have all loosened as you have exhaled away tension and anxiety.
Good.
Notice this sensation of calm and relaxation your body is experiencing.
This is a benefit you can partake of anywhere that you are.

Breathing in through your nose, into your diaphragm and filling your lungs then slowly exhaling away the tension you have held, giving way to relaxation and peace.

This process allows you to focus on cleansing your body and releasing it from anxiety so that you can experience the light, easy feeling of calm.

Let's take another breath, in through your nose, filling up the diaphragm and lungs.

Pause.

Slowly exhale until all the air has gone.

Now breathe normally.

Remember this feeling, this sensation of relaxation This is a place you can return to whenever you need it.

Now, whenever you are ready you can open your eyes and stretch, taking with you all the benefits of relaxation.

Worry docs not empty tomorrow of it's sorrow,
It empties today of its strength.
-Corrie Ten Boom

CONCLUSION

I was blessed with an exceptional and immense support system. I decided early on in my cancer journey that I would not hold back about my life in the midst of cancer and would be transparent in hopes of encouraging others on their journey, but also as a way to let people in my circle know what kind of support I needed. People won't know how to aid you if you don't tell them.

I'm not foolish enough to think that everyone in the world who will be diagnosed with cancer or any other life-changing illness or disease will have the strong supports that I have had. So if you find yourself in a position where you are lacking social supports I have a couple ideas for you:

Join a support group.

Truly, this is a wonderful way to connect with people who are on the same healing journey as you. Everyone will be in a different place on that journey, but it will always help to connect with people of similar experience. If your local hospital does not host support groups, check with the American Cancer Society (their website is on the resource page in this booklet). If there is no support group in your area, the ACS often has mentors available, those who have gone through cancer treatment and who have volunteered to be contacted by newly diagnosed individuals for the purpose of support and information.

Join a spiritual community.

If you are not already part of a church, temple, mosque, or synagogue, then now may be the perfect time for you to find one. Some spiritual communities have house groups or small groups that may be a more intimate way for you to become involved. Perhaps you would prefer the anonymity of the larger church service. That would be fine initially, but the idea here is to become integrated, not to remain a bystander. Build relationships, share your story, provide support, and allow yourself to be supported in return.

I truly hope the things you have read here will be of encouragement to you. Any new diagnosis can be frightening, but if we can put it in perspective as a matter of imbalance or dis-ease in our body, take time to breathe, "get our ducks in a row," and build a supportive team, this should give us the courage to make decisions most genuine to who we are…choices that take us on a peaceful path.

Please use the rest of this workbook as a record-keeping resource. I've provided a sample page as to how it might be utilized at your appointments and left the rest blank for you to use however you'd like. I hope you find it a useful tool in the days ahead.

Blessings to you, Reader.

We can't direct the wind,
But we can adjust the sails.
Thomas S. Monson

EXAMPLE

(How I use the form.)

Who DR.WHO

What ULTRASOUND LEFT KNEE CAP

Where ST. MARY'S HOSPITAL, KANKAKEE

When FEBRUARY 1, 1996

Notes:

Medication changed to 2x a day. Told doctor about change in appetite.

Doctor gave us the name of a nutritionist: Kelli Bonomo 800-555-1212.

Signed up for patient portal and wrote details in the back.

(Or)Received a copy of the blood work report. (Or both!)

Next appointment is Saturday, February 12th.

Who ____

What ____

Where ____

When ____

Notes:

____

____

____

____

____

____

____

____

____

____

____

____

____

____

____

Who ____

What ____

Where ____

When ____

Notes:

Who ____

What ____

Where ____

When ____

Notes:

____

____

____

____

____

____

____

____

____

____

____

____

____

____

____

Who ____

What ____

Where ____

When ____

Notes:

Who ______________________________

What ______________________________

Where ______________________________

When ______________________________

Notes:

____
____
____
____
____
____
____
____
____
____
____
____
____
____
____

Who ______________________________

What ______________________________

Where ______________________________

When ______________________________

Notes:

Who ____

What ____

Where ____

When ____

Notes:

Who ____________________

What ____________________

Where ____________________

When ____________________

Notes:

Who ______________________________

What ______________________________

Where ______________________________

When ______________________________

Notes:

Who ______________________________

What ______________________________

Where ______________________________

When ______________________________

Notes:

Who ____

What ____

Where ____

When ____

Notes:

Who ____

What ____

Where ____

When ____

Notes:

____

____

____

____

____

____

____

____

____

____

____

____

____

____

____

Who ______________________________

What ______________________________

Where ______________________________

When ______________________________

Notes:

Who ____

What ____

Where ____

When ____

Notes:

Who ____

What ____

Where ____

When ____

Notes:

Who ______________________________

What ______________________________

Where ______________________________

When ______________________________

Notes:

Who ____

What ____

Where ____

When ____

Notes:

Who ____

What ____

Where ____

When ____

Notes:

Who ____

What ____

Where ____

When ____

Notes:

____

____

____

____

____

____

____

____

____

____

____

____

____

____

____

Who ______________________________

What ______________________________

Where ______________________________

When ______________________________

Notes:

Who ____

What ____

Where ____

When ____

Notes:

Who ____

What _______________________________________

Where ______________________________________

When _______________________________________

Notes:

Who ____

What ____

Where ____

When ____

Notes:

Who ______________________________

What ______________________________

Where ______________________________

When ______________________________

Notes:

Who ____

What ____

Where ____

When ____

Notes:

____

____

____

____

____

____

____

____

____

____

____

____

____

____

____

Who ____

What ____

Where ____

When ____

Notes:

Who ____

What ____

Where _______________________________________

When ____

Notes:

Who ____

What ____

Where ____

When ____

Notes:

Who ____

What ____

Where ____

When ____

Notes:

Who ____

What ____

Where ____

When ____

Notes:

Who ____

What ____

Where ____

When ____

Notes:

____

____

____

____

____

____

____

____

____

____

____

____

____

____

____

Who ____

What ____

Where ____

When ____

Notes:

Who ______________________________

What ______________________________

Where ______________________________

When ______________________________

Notes:

____

____

____

____

____

____

____

____

____

____

____

____

____

____

____

Who ______________________________

What ______________________________

Where ______________________________

When ______________________________

Notes:

Who ______________________________

What ______________________________

Where ______________________________

When ______________________________

Notes:

____

____

____

____

____

____

____

____

____

____

____

____

____

____

____

Who ____

What ____

Where _______________________________________

When ____

Notes:

Who ______________________________

What ______________________________

Where ______________________________

When ______________________________

Notes:

Who ____

What ____

Where ____

When ____

Notes:

Who ____

What ____

Where ____

When ____

Notes:

Who ____

What ____

Where ____

When ____

Notes:

Who ____

What ____

Where ____

When ____

Notes:

Who ____

What ____

Where ____

When ____

Notes:

Who ______________________________

What ______________________________

Where ______________________________

When ______________________________

Notes:

Who ____

What ____

Where ____

When ____

Notes:

Who ______________________________

What ______________________________

Where ______________________________

When ______________________________

Notes:

Who ______________________________

What ______________________________

Where ______________________________

When ______________________________

Notes:

Who ______________________________

What ______________________________

Where ______________________________

When ______________________________

Notes:

Who ____

What ____

Where ____

When ____

Notes:

Who ____

What ____

Where ____

When ____

Notes:

____

____

____

____

____

____

____

____

____

____

____

____

____

____

____

MEDICATION/SUPPLEMENT LIST

Medication/Supplement	Prescribing Doctor	Dosage
An Apple	Dr. Who	~~2 per day~~
"	"	1 per day
Sunshine	Dr. Feelgood	2 hours a day
ETC.		

MEDICATIONS/SUPPLEMENT LIST

Medication/Supplement	Prescribing Doctor	Dosage

MEDICATIONS/SUPPLEMENT LIST

Medication/Supplement	Prescribing Doctor	Dosage

PATIENT PORTAL KEY

Portal Location	User Name	Password
StMarysHospital.com	Patient#1	Thriver32
Generalhospital.com	Myname1	Breathe32
Etc.		

All shall be well, and all shall be well

and all manner of things shall be well.

-Julian of Norwich